Sounds Easy
Vowel Sound 'a'

Sounds Easy Series

Copyright © Egon Publishers Ltd
and Rosalind Birkett, 1993
Second impression 1997
Third impression 2001

ISBN 0 905858 65 4

Designed by Howard Birkett,
Amaryllis Software Ltd, Berkhamsted, Herts

Printed by Streetsprinters, Baldock, Herts

Published by
Egon Publishers Ltd
Royston Road, Baldock, Herts SG7 6NW

TEACHERS' NOTES

LEVEL 0. PRE-READING BOOKS

These books have been designed to help children with visual sequential memory difficulties. They draw attention to the vowels 'a', 'o', 'i', 'e' and 'u' (in that order). First say the word to the pupil and talk about the picture. The pupil should then trace each letter with a finger, saying the letter sound at the same time and finally say the whole word. Point out the highlighted vowel.

INTRODUCTORY LEVEL AND LEVEL 1. FIRST READING BOOKS

Can be used as a reading scheme, or as supplementary books to Spelling Made Easy, 'Fat Sam' – Introductory Level and 'Sam and the Tramp' – Level 1 (Violet Brand). They gradually introduce new vowel sounds, reinforcing the word families.

Acknowledgements

Special thanks to John and Heather Adkins, the staff and children of Egerton-Rothesay Lower School, Berkhamsted, to Violet Brand for her encouragement and inspiration and of course to my family, Lucy (for Ted), Joanna (for Top the Frog) and my husband Howard, without whom these books would not have been written.

Sounds Easy Series

ROSALIND BIRKETT

Level 0   Book 1

Vowel Sound 'a'

EGON PUBLISHERS LTD

mat

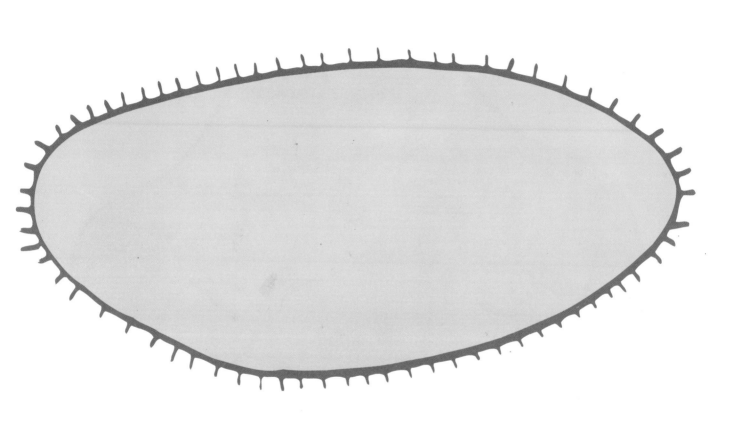

sad

pan

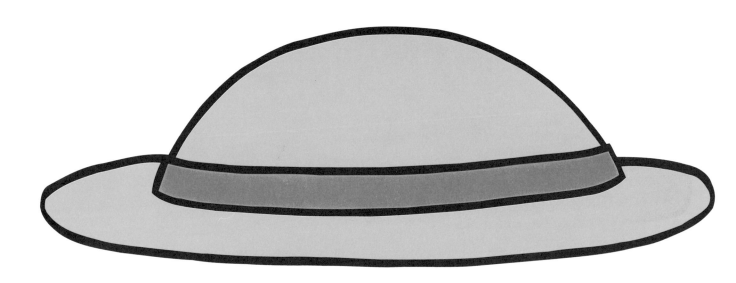

hat

man

cat

ham

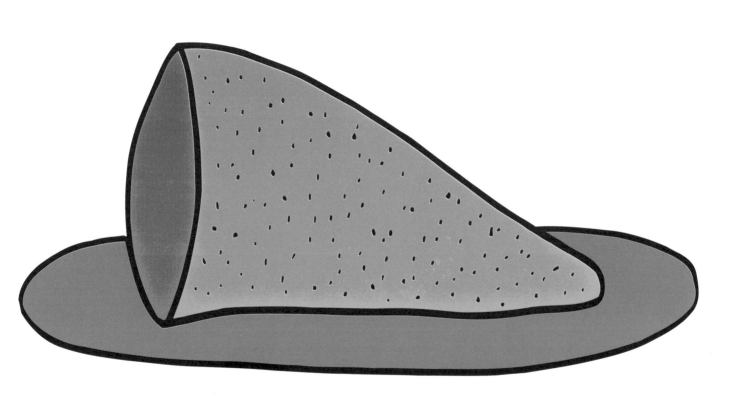